To Cheryl and Stan,
Thanks for "Being There"
Dave + Ruth Boons

A WALK IN THE WOODS
THE TALE OF RUDY BOOTS
DAVID CHARLES GOSSE

"THOUGH HE HAS FOUR PAWS, A DOG CAN ONLY WALK ONE PATH"

4 Pause Publishing

Copyright © 2011
 by David Charles Gosse

Photographs © 2011
 by David Charles Gosse

All rights reserved.

No part of this book may be used or reproduced in any manner without the written permission of the Publisher.

ISBN-13: 978-1456345341
ISBN-10: 1456345346

Published by 4 Pause Publishing
       dcgphoto@gci.net

Dedicated To

Shadow dado, Kovu Roi, Sara Bea and Mom

Acknowledgments:

Editor: Karen S. Davis
www.KarenSDavis.com

Production Coordination: Joanne Bolton
www.boltonprinting.com

Production: Deborah Perdue
www.illuminationgraphics.com

And to Perry Merkel and Café del Mundo where they graciously let my dad sit for hours polishing my poetry.

Prologue

Anyone who has ever strolled through the woods will likely be able to relate to this little book. On your walks you have probably spotted some trees that look strangely like something else. Maybe it's just the way the light hits them, or the angle of viewing, or maybe a bit of both. Whatever the setting, don't you often find yourself saying "Look at that! That tree looks just like a duck, or a bear, or my Aunt Helen. I wish I had my camera!" These days it would be more like, I wish I had my phone, or pen or some other multi-purpose device that also takes photos.

Well my little dog Rudy Boots encounters these "aberrations" quite often on our walks in Kincaid, a rustic park near our home in Anchorage, Alaska. They scare him and so he turns and trots (he **never** runs) in the opposite direction. That direction is usually away from the other dogs and me. So, what *was* a leisurely walk, becomes a game of "go fetch"...Rudy that is.

Tired of being accused of losing his way, or having an overactive imagination, Rudy decided to take matters into his own paws and went into action. He went after the proof to show what frightens him really does exsist. Determined to interview these "monsters" as he calls them, he took a notepad, our jeep and one of my cameras and set off into the woods. His thought was to write a best-selling book to clear his name...and perhaps make a little extra money because he knows that, while the coffee appears to him to be free at the coffee stands we frequent, the dog bones can be quite expensive!

So this is his story as he told it to me. He speaks in rhyme as he says "all doggies do," and has mentioned that it might be better if the book is *barked* out loud instead of simply read silently.

Whatever you decide, we hope you enjoy it.

David Charles Gosse
Anchorage, Alaska
2011

Note: All of the images in this book are exactly as Rudy "took" them, with minor enhancements such as dodging and burning.

Devil's Club – *the villain in our story*

-noun

a green shrub with maple-shaped leaves similar to nettles of the west and east coast of North America. Thriving in the dark, damp areas of Alaska the plant can form in vast thickets with stems growing up to ten feet and cause havoc for anyone who comes into contact with it. Devil's Club is the local name for this flora known as *Echinopanax horridus* in the Latin or technical term. *Echino* refers to

the spiny thorns which inject a formic acid "juice" up to 1/4" into it's victim causing a stinging sensation, *panax* from the Greek panakos (a panacea) in reference to it's medicinal uses, and *horridus* which is self-evident from the festering of the "invisible" needles which are hard to dig out and can cause severe pain. And so we begin...

I am Rudy of Boots, for whom the crowd roots
And for me all the ladies do pine.
Noble of birth, I was set on this Earth
Through no fault (or decision) of mine.

By many names I am known, into some I have grown
But of several I'm not a fan.
I am *Booty-Bob* down in Texas, *Baddy-Boo* in my Lexus
And *Rudy-like-Boo-ta* in Japan.

Mr. Peabody I find springs to the mind
Of a forty-plus-old 'Boomer's' head.
But *My Liege* I prefer (at the very least *Sir*)
Or simply, *Your Eminence*, instead.

Though a master of wit, I'll go easy on it
As I speak of things hard to relate.
But enough about me, for in time you will see
Why I seem to the masses so great.

"Mr. Peabody"

Some say I am witty. Some say I am pretty.
Inspired, they follow my path.
Those less enlightened (more likely just frightened)
Consider my wit only half.

Now to the business at hand-there appears in my land
A park known to all as Kincaid.
Here daily I go, with my siblings in tow
Where several small piles are made.

Our dad armed with bags, our sculptures he snags
While I aimlessly change my direction.
Boots dawdles and rambles, his thinking's a shambles-
"Doggie-mentia" may be his affliction.

I see things here and there that are hard to put square
My peers think my life is amiss.
They all think I'm a loo-loo, all filled up with doo-doo
But you see, from my tale, I digress.

If you *could* hear me speak, you might think me a freak
It's your mind, it's too busy I fear.
Doggies talk all the time, quite often in rhyme
But here, I'll write it out, so it's clear.

And so for the masses (those lads and those lasses
Who need solid proof to believe),
Photos by Boots, with words fast and loose
I go into the woods to retrieve.

I tend to be lionized, so I must not be recognized
Should my findings come under a cloud.
So I don a disguise, and the time that it buys
While I'm weaving my way through the crowd.

They may think I'm my dad, which would be rather sad
Though our features they say are the same.
Both short and both white (a phenomenal sight!)
We diverge in the reach of our fame.

With these blocks on my feet, which look rather neat
I shall motor myself to the Portal.
No seatbelt I need, for on danger I feed!
They'll see I'm no ordinary mortal.

I now have the key, but gas is not free
So I pinch just a bit of Dad's cash.
On my way I'll soon be, but first I must pee
Then off to my destiny dash.

Soon enough you'll discover that I work undercover
My passport, to the right, you can see.
No one knows who I am, so I shall call myself "Sam"
And only *I* will know that it's me.

Two paws on the wheel, no pedals I feel
I'd be taller, I think, if I stood.
But I slouch in the seat, metal 'neath my "blocked" feet
I go low-riding out of our 'hood.

Rudy "Bond"

Adjusting the mirror, I glance at who's in there
It's Bond. Rudy Bond, I dare say.
Shaken not stirred, deadly charm in a word
Call me vain, I just can't look away.

I feel cars whizzing by (not sufficiently high
To look out and observe where I'm going).
If I crash (and I could), our insurance is good
And I know last year Dad added towing.

So I finally arrive (by chance still alive)
And the Portal I spy straight ahead.
I lose the glasses and hat, put on Dad's baseball cap
I've become Sam, the "dog tourist" instead.

With camera in paw, I shall shoot what I saw
All my pens, they are chewed pencil sharp.
My license scratched clean (cops know what I mean)
I am finally ready to start.

The Portal

Have you pondered the "they" about whom many say
"We must listen, their judgment is true!"
But if you stepped back a bit, and tried using your wit
You would see that these "theys" have no clue!

You see, mysteries abound-they exist all around
And to grasp them our brains we must tap.
Like when from a seat, you arise to your feet
Where goes that thing called your lap?

Of course Portals are rare (especially if they're not there)
But the one in the picture is clear.
And I'll say, if I dare, past that threshold is where
Lie the demons I so often fear.

They're medieval distortions in rather large portions
I spy them when we're out on our walks.
All cropped and deformed and repeatedly scorned
Cloistered secrets of which no one talks.

I am told they're illusions, their scrapes and contusions
Are easily etched in the wood.
But with just the right light, they can toy with one's sight
And "they" say they won't harm, but they could.

So then this is my quest (for this task, I'm the best-
I'm not bragging, just no one else cares).
While they're having a nap, their depictions I'll snap
I will catch them within their own snares.

Then their stories I'll nab (standing too far to grab
And for fear of their hypnotic look).
Then I'll find my way back, to my point of attack
To start writing a best-selling book.

All of my senses in all of their tenses
Tell me I should turn around.
So I sally forth senseless, maintaining my tenseness
Stepping out onto forbidden ground.

Where no dog's gone before! My name written in lore!
I have burned all my ships...except two.
As I go into the fog, that's one small step for dog
One giant leap over bear poo.

I encountered this bear and tried not to stare
But he's the first "fear" I ever saw.
He'd squash *me* like a bug, then I'd be *his* rug!
Did you notice the size of that paw?

I said "Hey there, good-lookin'!" and "Whatcha got cookin'?"
(I hoped that it wouldn't be me).
He looked all around and then down at the ground
When he sensed me I started to pee.

But he couldn't observe me- bad eyesight you see
I kept still and away from his wrath.
He growled, "What do you want, my annoying piss-ant?
Are you closing what's left of my path?"

Mr. Bear

"Well that's not very friendly," I said very gently
Though I must say I did use a tone.
"Would you rather I left you forlorn and bereft?
Desert you and leave you alone?"

"No one comes near," he said, "from here they steer clear
There's not one soul with whom I can play.
Though conceited you seem, you do *look* like ice cream
So I really would like you to stay.

"I remember a time when my path was a line
And all sorts of fine playmates would pass.
Then *they* altered its source (it's now an obstacle course!)
Which has left me alone and quite crass."

"But you're a wonderful bear! I'll return to your lair
And we'll play there late into the night."
"And you are a fine goat," he did kindly emote
"On that day all that's *left* will be *right*."

"You speak nicely today, now my friend, can you say
Are there others like you I may see?"
"That old smart-aleck frog," he said, "down in the bog
Someone backslapped him into a tree.

"Be careful my new friend, for their cruelty may descend
On your sensitive soul, and I fear-
They'll make you so mean, with their senseless machine
You will never more want to play here."

"Oh, that never could be. I'll come back here, you'll see!"
I was *up* as I went *down* the road.
No need to steer clear, for I had nothing to fear
From a smart-aleck, backslapped old toad.

So just who are these "they" who I heard the bear say
Had turned him so bitter and cold?
Perhaps this poor toad, I can possibly goad
To shed light on things yet to be told.

"Why hello Mister Frog, your face goes *well* with that log"
He really just looked like a splat.
"I have now just awoke…"(I sensed pain as he spoke)
"Do come closer, my white fashion rat."

"Fashion rat indeed! This from you I don't need!
My dimensions are three to your two!"
He croaked, "Please don't be cross, for I'm at such a loss
I've no notion of what I'm to do.

"The details are complex, and please call me Alex
For you I can hear, but not see.
Laws of physics hold true, for a being in two
There's no you, who lives out 'there' in three."

This was no normal frog. Take a tip from this dog
He was *sharp*, even though he was *flat*.
"Our wit they call callous, because we are smart, Alex
Now say, who moved your front to your back?"

Alex

"Flora green, lean, and mean- a destructive machine
They had holes where their souls used to live.
They were friendly at first, but it only got worse
What they did I can never forgive.

"*'Froggie, tell us some way we can ruin your day'*
Their distainful approach sent me south.
I went slightly insane and bypassing my brain
An 'Up yours!' escaped from my mouth.

"What followed that out of my ungoverned snout
Was a blast of wit fit for a king.
But they had little use for my royal abuse
I said, 'Kiss it!' (not meaning my ring).

"They asked, *'Are you a prince?'* I said, now, past, or since?
Now consulting each other they sighed.
*'Oh, this mouth we must ban. He belongs in a pan
And so, Mister Toad, you are fried!'*

"Then my rear they did tap, and there put a cap
And I flew through the air, it was wild!
Ah, my life I could mend, if that cap were the end
But this tree, thinks of me, as her child!

Alex sent me to Easter Man, who's real name was Stan
Was my goal now a man or a basket?
But there he was by a tree, as the toad did decree
A mummy alone with no casket.

"Hello Mister E," I proposed cheerfully
"May I please take a photo or two?"
"Who speaks in this way?" he struggled to say
"Have you come here to take me with you?"

"Where on earth would we go?" I was yearning to know
"Well," he said, "to my tribe on the Rock.
I would now be resettled, had those devils not meddled
I slept here as away flew my flock."

I knew of the place that has face after face
From the tabletop books no one reads.
A bunch of stone heads, upright in their beds
Prime real estate covered in weeds.

It would cause quite a stir if I said his friends were
Time-sharing where bunnies lay eggs.
"You've a much better space, in this radiant place
Just look! You have still got your legs!

"How did you get here? By what star did you steer?"
I quizzed him, "What sent you astray?"
"We walked over a bridge-an east-westerly ridge
A million years past to the day."

My new friend, it seems, lived too much in his dreams
He'd been dozing for quite a long time.
His reason got wilted and his reality tilted
He was clearly long past his prime.

Stan

"I haven't my ticket-it's lost in this thicket
I need it to fly south to my Isle.
But my little white pig, I have no arms to dig
Would you stay here and help me awhile?"

"I would love to help look, but I must finish my book
See, my agent can be rather harsh.
But if *you* wouldn't mind, please helping *me* find
The quickest way out of this marsh."

"If you say you won't stay, then I bid you good day
And no more of my time shall you steal.
Go see the Croc in the Wood"-what I now understood
Was my quest had become an ordeal.

That guy was alright, though a little uptight
If *I* had friends who left, *I'd* be sore.
But he's clearly ahead, and the same can't be said
Of all those who will never be more.

Easter Island sounds strange, this they should change
To a name that much better suits.
A description with flair, elegance, savoir-faire
Something subtle, like *The Isle of Boots!*

A resort in the tropics, for those with deep pockets
French poodles, grass skirts on their booty.
And I must have I say, my own holiday
I think I shall call it *ThanksRudy!*

I detected his head, with a log for a bed
He was frozen in time like a fossil.
A force in his day, he now held little sway
That said, he was not all that docile.

"Howdy-doo, Gator-head," I most pleasantly said
"Mister Easter Egg sends you his best!"
"Yes, I heard you were here," he returned with a sneer
"They said to look for a pale, pompous pest."

"What on earth did I do, besides talking to you
That has put such a bee in your bonnet?
Like the 'basket' back there, you be nice, or I swear
I will write you right out of this sonnet!"

Henceforth acting his age (to stay on the page)
He asked, "What do would you want me to do?"
"You could give a line and some pics would be fine
That's the most I am asking of you."

"My manners are gone," he said, "and my patience is none
You can see I'm impaled to this tree.
It wasn't always like this, at one time it was bliss
It's my fate, this is how it must be."

"Why say that you're through? There must be someone to sue!
You're *right*, you've been *wronged*, that's a fact!"
"Ah, this play's nearly done," he moaned, "the villains have won
Unless a hero arrives in this act.

Alberto

"For now visit Fifi, on an invite from me
Say Alberto Ebon said to see her."
For this nice-sounding wench, I'll bone up on my French!
"See you later, my friend, Al E. Gator."

So I got myself set, to woo a coquette
All pretty, perfumed and refined.
Little did I know, that at the end of my 'bow
What a black pot of coal I would find.

"My vanilla cream cone," came a syrupy tone
"I have heard from the group of your quest.
Your good looks I have eyed, now come sit by my side
Draw closer and be dear Fifi's guest."

With her eyes buggy red, and those horns on her head
It was easy resisting her charms.
Reminiscent somehow, of a misguided cow
I stayed just out of reach of those arms.

Fifi

The smell of her breath nearly scared me to death
From her slurring I knew she was 'lit'.
"You, my sweet snowy ball, our past love can recall?"
I felt sure that just *couldn't* be it.

"You are hardly exotic-you seem completely robotic
A cartoon of metal and wire."
"Oh, my silver-haired Jacques, that silver-tounged talk
Is a treat I so often desire.

"Do remain with me here as my steady Pierre
May I pour you a glass of snail slime?"
"More than tempted I am," said this quivering Sam
"But perhaps, my dear, some other time."

"Then be gone from my sight, you white parasite!
Of your presence I now grow fatigued!"
So I clicked in a hurry, backed off from her fury
Quite flattered, but more so, relieved.

I got clear of the smell but could still hear her yell
"I forgive you my albino snot!"
Not taking the bait, my laissez-faire gait
Turned into a terrorized trot.

Now a scent filled the air (not of Fifi I swear!
Whose perfume, *Desperation*, floats far).
It was manly and tough, somewhat gracious, yet gruff
The smell of a two-bit cigar.

A new horror I found, coming out of the ground
A man who looked rough for his years.
Appealing he was not, for he'd been punched in a lot
And will you get a load of those ears!?

"Ahoy and Aweigh," seemed the right thing to say
He struck me a bit of a sailor.
His shifting cigar, his nose left ajar
His body, gone in search of a tailor.

This face without legs was a carton of eggs
All bumpy, and bulbous, and brown.
I kept that to myself, (I'm a smart little elf
It's too soon to be run out of town).

"Step up on my wharf, my snow-white dwarf
What brings you to walk on my span?"
He seemed friendly I'd say, in a *nightmarish* way
He went by the name of Lou Tan.

"Let us skip to my Lou, why I've come to see you
I seek stories to fill my new book.
I need proof you exsist. I must really insist
For you seem to have just the right look."

"Go ahead, snap away, but don't take all day
Let the planet perceive how I am.
I'm resigned to a fate, to which few can relate
Just be snappy, get snapping and scram!"

Lou

"Who are these 'they' Lou, that have done this to you?
Please reveal them so I might steer clear."
"'Tis the Club of the Devil, in misery they revel
Aye, *they* be the ones you should fear."

"Oh come now," I said, "this shrub's gone to your head"
But he answered with dread in his voice.
"When those flora have gone, we will all carry on
And the whole of this land shall rejoice."

"Who else knows of this weed, from whom all must be freed?
And who, other than you, had bad luck?"
"Just waddle down there," he said in despair
"You'll run into the body-less duck."

So I started to run, but Lou wasn't quite done
"Dwarf! His tale is a sad one indeed.
For it's not just the tail, that they dumped in the pail
But on his whole torso they feed.

"It is true we all grieve, but if ever they leave
And go back to the place where they burn.
Then we'll all be all right, what a wonderful sight
When *their* victims to normal return."

His voice faded away, and there in the road lay
The poor quacker of which he had spoke.
A frightening sight, just a head there alright
With my forepaw I gave it a poke.

"Hey, watch it there muff!" said the head in a huff
"Don't you think that I've been through enough?"
With that stick there and stuff, sticking out of his buff
What he'd been through must have been rough.

"What's left over of you," I proposed as if true
"Would turn many a sweet ducky's head."
"You dunce! I'm not male, but that's left in the pail
So I guess I am neither, instead."

I asked, "How could this be?" as I bent down to see
"What archfiend could do something so mean?"
"From hell they were sent!" and she said what she meant
"Blithely slicing and dicing me clean."

She looked fully filleted, a nice job they made
Putting all her best bits in the bucket.
Skinned to the bone, she was left here alone
Her poor head on a stick where they stuck it.

My book's theme I now see, the wrong genre may be
Of horror it screams, a la King.
But I can't change my course, I must get to the source
And there glimpse who could do such a thing.

"Please use your wit," she begged, "every least little bit
To drive this awful plague from our land.
If you'd be so kind, in awhile you may find
That best-selling book in your hand."

Miss Ducky

"Keep your head up my friend, for a paw I will lend
It appears you have none of your own."
"Go and see the cooked snake," she said, "down by the lake
And together a plan you can hone."

Was I hearing a moan? Perhaps more of a groan
Either way, what an unhappy sound!
Watching each little step, slowly onward I crept
Toward a snake, who's named Jake, on the ground.

I asked why he was blue. "What has happened to you?"
I did not really want a reply.
"It's those devils down there, that have caused my despair
They have torched me and left me to die."

Should this be in my book? It was worth a new look
Whether children should get this to read.
"So much carnage," I sighed, "like the toad, you are fried
This may not be the story I need."

Jake

"People want to read happy, sappy or crappy
Of heros that set others free.
But don't be confused, I will never be used
In a world that is not about me."

"But it *is* about you! And you know what is true!
Can you really deny what you saw?"
His words struck a chord, and my ship became moored
My enormous heart started to thaw.

"I will help you my friend, but why start at the end
Where the damage is already done?"
"It reverses," said he, "and we shall be set free
If *they* go back to where they've begun."

"But I am merely a cog, one brilliant white dog
And remarkable too, I must say.
As to what I can do, well, I haven't a clue
To covince them they must go away."

"Show them your wit," he said, "is preceded by 'nit'
And confused they will be all to hell.
Listening to you, they won't know what to do
They will see there's no gong in your bell."

Well this snake was quite smart-he was sharp as a dart
To discern such potential in me.
"I am Hell among Hounds!" (I do like how that sounds)
"Yes, your hero, my briquette, I will be.

"I am eager to go, but first, I must know
Are they sure to be swayed by my charm?"
He assured, "You can depend, they will notice my friend
That your horses have all left the barn."

As he gave me a shove, I heard a voice from above
"To go past here you must pay a fee."
I recognized the tone, as if it came from a clone
For it sounded exactly like me!

"It is I!" I yelled out, "Are the devils about?
I have interest in 'shooting' the Club."
"My silly white lass," it said, "you never shall pass
And therein, you see, lies the rub."

Then I looked up on high, and aloft I did spy
A kitty, just as cruel as they come.
Well if this be my foil, then I shall not recoil
I'd stand fast (though I'd much rather run).

"Before you can go, I must let you know
A riddle of mine you must solve.
While the answer is here, it must be perfectly clear
Around this, does your whole fate revolve!"

"Then do what you do, I have no fear of you
For my wit is the equal of yours.
Bring it on! Give your best! I am up to the test!
You forget that I walk on all fours."

Kitty

"Picture then, if you will, a glass I half fill
With some water refreshing and cool.
My question to you-tell me what's true-
Half empty, that glass, or half full?"

I thought with my head, then confronting her said
"Well, it really is neither you see.
I don't mean to sass, but the mass of the glass
Is clearly twice the size it should be."

I could tell my refrain had disordered her brain
"Oh my! No one's said *that* before.
Though there was no solution, you found resolution
The devils are going to be sore.

"If you follow this road to their gaudy abode
You will see them injecting their stew."
"I am up to the task," I said, "but before I go I must ask
How on earth did they do this to you?"

"Well I really can't tell-they'd be *hotter* than hell!
And for me there would be no parole."
"This *is* a curse!" I cried, "but what could be worse
Than your head in a woodpecker hole?"

There they were, straight ahead, like the mouser had said
All greenish and morbid of form.
More close I must look at this crux of my book
Yet careful to not tempt their scorn.

The smaller, named Luce, was injecting their "juice"
In the neck of the one named Korfu.
When they saw my chagrin, and my "Cheshire Cat" grin
Vanish, is what I wished *I* could do.

They sang "Why so giddy, my little white pretty?
Our party's just beginning to start."
Thoughts of Toto in the basket, then me in a casket!
I knew now, how I shall, play this part.

"It's Margaret Hamilton I hear in your cynical sneer"
Their heads shook, they'd no clue who she was.
"She played the witch and old biddy, from the Emerald City
In that kid flick *The Wizard of Oz*.

"'I'm melting! I'm melting! Toto is helping
Where are all my monkeys with wings!?'
I'm really suprised, that with all of your spies
You're so badly informed about things.

"You aren't looking so stout, you should really get out
Maybe take a dance lesson or two.
Or teach yourselves cricket, oh yes, that's the ticket-
Learn a game of which few have a clue."

Well, they were *not* amused-perhaps bewildered, confused
So I stared down my snout with distain.
"He's superior to us," they conversed, "so let's not make a fuss
It's clear this white rabbit's got game."

The "Club"

I chirped, "This is the end, we will not meet again
Unless on your lake I can skate."
"Is he all that he seems? We know not what he means
Such a creature we cannot debate."

"You're melting! You're melting! This white dog is helping
No sign of those bullies with wings.
Do you want some more pain? I can taunt you again
I know lots of nonsensical things."

"No! Quit it! Enough! You've called out our bluff
Our circuits are fried-every one!
Others senseless like you, we must study a few
We'll be back!" and like that, they were gone!

I stood there awhile and then started to smile
When a thundering roar did I hear.
As I looked all around for the source of the sound
What it was became suddenly clear.

It was every loose end who was now on the mend
Free at last as their captors took flight.
Things were back like before, with the devils no more
So they hugged every white dog in sight.

"It was over like that!" said the now prancing cat
"You dropped them one round in the ring!"
"That old skin I have shed," the snake slithered and said
"I would hug you but that's not my thing."

"I've legs, thighs and breast!" the duck hugged my chest
Then she continued her running amuck.
"And my face is all clean," Lou Tan said with a beam
"In my pockets, my hands I can tuck!"

"Well you sure used your noodle," said Fifi the poddle
Now all pretty, dressed up and refined.
I felt claws on my back, but this was no attack
Just Al Gator with a hug from behind.

Then my Easter Clan Man, with plane ticket in hand
Shook my paw with the other and said-
"I love you little dog, for you have freed this old log
Here I come, Easter Island Club Med!"

Ah, but what of the toad? "Let's go on down the road!"
Froggie croaked, as he sat on my rear.
I said, "My little webbed friend, you've your pond to attend
I must go it alone now from here."

With his path now all right, and his refurbished sight
"I have no words," Bear said with a sigh.
As his paws drew me near, the best friend I'd made here
Held me close and then started to cry.

"I will miss you the most," I declared to my host
"You were nicest to me, this I know.
I wish I could stay on your new path and play
But back home, to my own, I must go."

Lost Rudy

Then I heard them all say, "Let's establish a day
To remember our buddy, Sir Booty!
That you leave we regret, but we'll never forget
Once a year, we will cheer, on *ThanksRudy*!"

"Had you not come our way, we would not have this day
We would love to do something for you!"
"I am lost, this I fear-my way home isn't clear
As to which path to take, I've no clue."

"Though you're far from your home, you are never alone
We are here for you now if you need.
But alas and alack, we don't know *your* way back
It's to *our* homes that all these roads lead."

"The *Madame* in the tree! That is who he should see"
Said Fifi, as a matter of fact.
"Ah, *mon cheri*, she is much wiser than we
She will know how to get you on track.

That she knows up from down, there's no getting around
But my path is already too long.
So my dad I shall call with this cell in my paw
Just in case the tree pointed me wrong.

Blast! No bars in the park, and not long before dark
I *find* I have no time to *lose*.
With few options in sight, on their cheers I took flight
In search of the road I should choose.

I trudged back and forth, to the south and then north
Their directions, better *left*, than were *right*.
Then there in the tree, what a beauty was she
But if her *bark* isn't good, that will *bite*.

"Little one, I am here. There is no need to fear."
She expressed as if saving the day.
"You are frozen in wood," I said as nice as I could
"How can *you* assist *me* on *my* way?"

"Try not to be rude, my fair-haired little dude
Take the 'fish' off your 'self' and add 'less.'"
Had she tried to be clever? A fruitless endeavor
What she meant was, I'm selfish, I guess.

"It's not all about you, which you know to be true
That is why you still wear your mask.
You fear others will show, answers you may not know
So, like directions, no questions you ask.

"As for how you must go, that way I don't know
For I'm simply a tree dripping sap.
Only the Angel is real, express to her what you feel
If you're true, she will show you the map."

Now I feel truly alone (I've no map and no phone
And no one to point out the way),
Yet I feel strangely akin, to my very own skin
Yes, somehow, I'm now feeling okay.

Madame

The tree said ask then I'll know, what others can show
I was once certain *I* knew it all.
But once I was *one*, and now I am *some*
I have friends now on whom I can call.

I was not one to ask, just went on wearing my mask
One asks only if one knows the answer.
It was the lawyer in me, but how much happier I'd be
If I'd spent all my life as a dancer.

Then into my sight came a brilliant white light
A one-hundred-foot Angel. Egad!
If I ask her sincerely, perhaps she will hear me
And point out the path back to my dad.

Though her halo shone bright, I had no fear of flight
I felt tasked, when she asked, what I'd learned.
"I know I need others help, it's no good by myself
And that love, like lost dogs, be returned.

The Angel

"What we see is not *all*, on this blue spinning ball
Some answers must be felt to be seen.
For if these feelings I trust, (and trust is a must)
There's no end to the insights I'll glean.

"But my worst fear has been, from the dirt I begin
I'm alone, and when I die, dirt I'll be.
And when I'm gone I'll feel sad, but if I'm sad, then I'm glad
For if I *feel*, then I'm *real*, now I see."

"You *do* see now my friend," she said, "that you never *do* end
And what you *do*, or don't *do* is a choice.
Choose to help others my dear, and help for you will appear
You have found your way home, so rejoice.

"Always follow your bliss and your life won't be amiss
You have friends now, you see that's the key."
What she said *felt* so right, and as I slept in her light
I knew, from my fears, I was free.

Found Rudy

Epilogue from Dad

My dog Rudy awoke when I gave him a poke
As he sat on my pack in the jeep.
With his pads colored blue (and his discs were full too)
He was quiet, so I knew he was beat.

Although he'd been bad, I can never stay mad
He relies upon this to be true.
Through our ups and our downs, as corny as it sounds
He's still my little dog, Rudy Boo.

Then I saw on his bling a most curious thing
With the tags 'round his neck was one more.
When I asked, "What is this here?"-I *saw* his eyes tear
Then I winked, and I *felt* his heart soar!

He looked up at me, as he gave me the key
I heard every word he *didn't* say.
I do love you Dad, and with you out ahead
I will never again lose my way.

As we drove off that day, there was no more to say
Rudy looked out the window and stared.
I was sure he would cry as some old trees we drove by
He was sad, but seemed no longer scared.

So get out of your 'hoods and take a walk in the woods
On this one special day every year.
It won't be very shrill, but if you remain still
You will hear his friend's *ThanksRudy!* cheer.

Thank You!

It was very nice of you to read my book.

"They" say a dog can't have an e-mail address,

but if you would like to contact me, please use my dad's:

dcgphoto@gci.net

Photos of me are also featured on my dad's website:

www.gosseimages.com

To purchase additional copies of my book, please visit the good folks at:

www.amazon.com

or
https://www.createspace.com/3500893
or
www.gosseimages.com

Made in the USA
Charleston, SC
05 June 2011